The Evolving Railway 1951-1976

Brian Morrison

crecy.co.uk

First published in 2020 by Crécy Publishing

A CIP record for this book is available from the British Library

Printed in Turkey by Pelikan Print

ISBN 978 1 90932 897 6

Crécy Publishing Limited
1a Ringway Trading Estate, Shadowmoss Road, Manchester M22 5LH
www.crecy.co.uk

FRONT COVER No 70002 *Geoffrey Chaucer* awaits departure from Liverpool Street on a misty evening. The crew have likely done all they can; boiler pressure just under maximum, coal pulled forward, boiler water well up in the glass and the footplate as clean and tidy as it was feasible to achieve on a steam engine. Perhaps the two men were enjoying a tea break at that moment. This type of turn was in the top-link for the men of Stratford, a long apprenticeship having been served before reaching the status of 'Express Driver'. Behind the engine, parcels and perhaps mails are being loaded but elsewhere all appears quiet. The pinpricks of light emerging from the headlamps are intended as a guide to staff as to the status of the train and certainly not designed to give any forward vision to the driver.

REAR COVER MAIN Framed in Gasworks Tunnel, New England (35A)-allocated Class V2 2-6-2 No 60966 powers the 9.00am boat train from King's Cross to Newcastle Tyne Commission Quay on 11 July 1953.

INSET TOP Having arrived at the WR station at Wolverhampton 'Low Level' with 'The Inter-City' express from Paddington on 20 July 1954, 'King' 4-6-0 No 6000 *King George V* is turned on the Stafford Road (84A) turntable in order to make the return journey.

INSET BOTTOM The 09.30 train to Cambridge winds out of Platform 2 at King's Cross on 12 June 1975, hauled by Class 31/4 No 31401.

TITLE PAGE A4 Pacific No 60014 Silver Link blasts away from King's Cross on 27 September 1953, and passes under the North London Line at Belle Isle, with the northbound 'Plant Centenarian', celebrating the centenary of Doncaster Works for the second week, the trains working in opposite directions.

Contents

Publisher's Introduction

The name Brian Morrison is one that will be familiar to at least three generations of railway photographers. Commencing his railway photography in 1951, his was a pictorial journey that continued for over sixty years until retiring from the scene a few years ago, this book concentrating on the years 1951 through to 1977. As such there are examples of steam and other motive power as well as train types and locations otherwise consigned to memory.

Railway editors of the time were quick to recognise a new talent and Brian had his first photograph published in October 1951. Since that time there have been countless others as well as several specific books from the stable of Messrs Ian Allan and OPC. Each of these followed a 'themed' topic likely set by the publisher but now for the first time Brian has free reign from his six-figure image library, choosing his own favourite views and stories to go with them.

What this new book contains are more than just images. Instead it is a wealth of memories for enthusiasts and observers. A personal and yet also public journey covering the length and breath of the mainland from a man who from the outset 'knew a good subject when he saw it'.

Now aged 90, Brian remains an enthusiast although now of the armchair type. He celebrated this milestone in March 2020 and looks forward to many more years recalling his hobby.

Brian Morrison's Railway Life
– The First 25 Years

My interest in railways began at school in 1942 when I was twelve years old and came about due to an annoyance with the procedures for school dinners, which in those days cost two shillings and sixpence (12½p) for the five-day week.

These dinners were held in differently timed sessions, each table of eight pupils being in the charge of a sixth-form prefect who undertook the serving. The regular prefect on my table was not a particularly pleasant boy by the name of Suddards but who was also referred by the nickname of 'Soapy'. Soapy's task was to dole out the food, supposedly equally amongst the eight on the table, but he always gave himself by far the largest portion of the food dishes, especially on 'chocolate pudding day' (Thursday) when he was particularly annoying by taking at least a quarter of the dish for himself, distributing the remainder in very small portions to the remaining eight of us on his table. Becoming more and more annoyed at his unfairness, I decided to join my classmates who did not partake in the school meals and cycled out with them to a field next to the local railway lines at Chislehurst, where we ate sandwiches provided by our mothers and watched the steam hauled Kent Coast expresses go by; for the most part ignoring the many electric multiple units operating to and from Charing Cross, Cannon Street and Victoria. Our group of about eight youngsters took the steam engine numbers and names of the variety of classes that included 'King Arthurs', 'Schools', 'L1's, 'E1's and 'D1's, etc and I was always given a cheer when 'King Arthur' No 782 *Sir Brian* went through!

In the same year, 1942, the first Ian Allan 'ABC of Southern Locomotives' was published, and the lists of numbers that we had already recorded in a variety of notebooks was transferred and duly underlined in the ABC as appropriate. The practice continued until the end of school days in 1946, when I joined the Railway Passengers Assurance Company, in the mistaken belief it was a part of the actual railway! It transpired that it was instead a subsidiary of the North British & Mercantile Insurance, later taken over by the Commercial Union Insurance Company. Nevertheless, I continued underlining in the now numerous Ian Allan ABCs and also travelled to various places all over the country until I was reluctantly conscripted to join the Army in 1948. It had been my intention to obtain a camera and commence recording the variety of locomotives that were in existence prior to Nationalisation, but this was just not possible as compulsory Army service did not end until 1951 when I was demobbed. With the Army gratuity received on release, I spent approximately half on an engagement ring for the young lady I had met while serving, and a further £19.50 on an Agfa Isolette camera that had a 1/500th second on the shutter speed. My first photograph was taken at Liverpool Street station in March 1951 and in the days when it had a large yard just outside the station, and is illustrated in this publication. Since then I have accumulated more than 200,000 views covering not just this country but also the USA and a number of European venues. The first to be published was in the October 1951 issue of *The Railway Magazine*, and, despite my interest in steam traction, was of the unique Bulleid diesel 0-6-0 No 11001 at Norwood Junction.

After that first photographic visit and also now having to work weekdays, I was more or less restricted to outings at weekends, but even so during the remainder of the year managed visits to Paddington, Waterloo (terminus), Clapham Junction, Charing Cross, Cannon Street, Bickley Junction, Chislehurst, Finsbury Park, Hadley Wood, Potters Bar, Norwood Junction and Eastleigh, some of the best of these also being shown in this publication. Various outings continued in 1952, and upon my marriage in June of that year, I visited the Isle of Wight on honeymoon. Not all of the two weeks there were spent in bed and I obtained some very nice photographs of both the Class 'O2' 0-4-4Ts on passenger workings and the 'E1' class 0-6-0Ts on freight! Thereafter I travelled over all parts of England, Scotland and Wales, and many of my favourite images are included herein, together with some from the ensuing twenty-four years.

On 7 March 1951, Class B17/1 'Sandringham' 4-6-0 No 61625 *Raby Castle* is serviced in the yard then just outside London Liverpool Street station. This was my first ever railway photograph taken with my first camera. A total of seventy-three of these three-cylinder engines were built between 1928 and 1937 and at the other end of the spectrum the first to go was in 1952 and the last in 1960. At the time of the photograph several of the class were engaged in working express services out of Liverpool Street - indeed the engine seen depicts a 'Class A' head code. They would be usurped from this type of duty soon after by the newly built 'Britannias'. None survived into preservation but a 'new-build' is under construction.

An immaculate A4 Pacific No 60028 *Walter K. Whigham* stands at King's Cross on 8 June 1961, waiting to depart with the 10.15 Royal Train to York. Royal train and other VIP workings were a prestige turn for the locomotive depot responsible for providing the motive power. For days if not weeks beforehand the running foreman would be considering the locomotive to use, usually one recently outshopped from works but also suitably run-in so any minor issues had been dealt with. Then there would be the matter of cleaning with literally days spent burnishing the selected engine 'to within an inch of its life'. This included not just what could be seen but also what could not be seen, the result a credit to all concerned even if most of the hard work would not be noticed by the travelling VIPs. Who for example would see the white painted cab roof, hardly practical with a steam loco but it was done all the same. The buffers are likely kept in store and especially fitted just for such an occasion although the same could not be said for the cylinder covers where an awful lot of elbow grease has been expended. The result would be that most of the shed staff from King's Cross (34A) would be outside watching their handiwork as the train passed on its journey north.

LEFT Standing beneath Sir John Hawkshaw's great crescent roof at Cannon Street station before it was torn down in April 1958, allegedly because it was unsafe due to wartime bomb damage, West Country Pacific No 34100 *Appledore* is at the head of an evening Ramsgate train on 25 April 1952. No 34100 was a long term Eastern Section locomotive but subsequently migrated to the Western Section of the Southern Region following rebuilding and the gradual elimination of steam on the lines in Kent. Seen from a low angle any steam locomotive is impressive by its sheer bulk, the original Bulleid breed (along with the A4) perhaps especially so due to their 'streamlined' appearance. The headcode discs here did not signify the type of train but on the Southern Region they referred instead to the route, so this Ramsgate train will be travelling via the Chislehurst Loop and Chatham.

BELOW Liverpool Street station is very different today to what it was when this scene was taken on 11 May 1951. With rays of spring sunshine manfully endeavouring to penetrate the sulphurous interior, Class N7/2 0-6-2T No 69681 awaits departure with a local service for Hertford East. Tank engines were as much a part of the London termini as were the main line engines, being employed on carriage shunting, station pilot, and as here on a local passenger working. It was only on the Southern Region where electric multiple units had almost totally usurped steam that they were less common although Victoria – Oxted and some Eastbourne workings out of Victoria were a common exception.

The 8.30am Crayford-Cannon Street via Sidcup service approaches its destination on 23 August 1951, formed of Class 4DD (double-deck) EMUs 4001 & 4002. The photographer was travelling on the train and the picture is taken from a carriage window at the rear. The smoke behind emanates from two Schools class and a D1 4-4-0. The idea of a double-deck train for the Southern came from the creative mind of Oliver Bulleid with just two four-car sets constructed. Whilst in theory the idea was sound there were issues with the wheels cracking – overcome – but dwell times at stations were more of a problem as the number of passengers now requiring to enter/exit from a set number of doors was never resolved. Ventilation in the upper compartments could have been cured with modern air-conditioning but more worrying were assaults on passengers who found themselves trapped on the upper level. That is not to say such events occurred continually but certainly during quieter times it was rare to find the seats in the upper deck occupied.

Marsh LBSCR Class I3 No 32091 on the manual turntable at New Cross Gate shed, 23 June 1951. Shunting stock in the yards to the rear is Billinton E3 class 0-6-2T No 32459. Steam engine working was certainly not all glamour, hard enough work on a dry day as here but in the face of a howling gale or freezing conditions it is plain to see why as years passed and cleaner, better paid jobs became available, men began to desert the railways. Add to that shift work and an engine such as this already well past its prime and life was certainly not easy. No 32091 would be withdrawn in June 1952 having spent its last few months of service allocated to Brighton.

28xx class 2-8-0 No 3860 near Twyford on 5 July 1951 heading for Oxley with a long rake of wooden-sided wagons. The headcode indicated an 'Express Freight' but not fitted with the continuous brake so meaning it would still be likely running at no more than 30mph and that dependent upon the gradient. Here at Twyford the line was almost level (a very gentle rise all the way from Paddington as far as Swindon) so the engine will be taking steam to pull the train. Even though it was designated as an 'Express', this was more a misnomer as the service would still be checked to allow faster services to pass especially once it had turned north at Didcot after which just two lines were available.

The last survivor of the L&SWR Drummond S11 class 4-4-0s, No 30400, under the coaling plant at Guildford (70C) shed on 1 September 1951; it would survive a further three years before it was finally condemned. Guildford shed was often regarded as the home to various locomotive types that had been pensioned off from duties elsewhere, indeed witness the Adams tender engine in the background and what appears to be another Adams design, an 'O2', behind No 30400. Guildford shed had responsibility for motive power on the goods and parcels services to Alton, goods and passenger workings down the Meon Valley route, the stub of the Tongham branch and also passenger and goods workings to Horsham.

Crossing the timber viaduct over the Langstone Channel to Hayling Island, the branch train from Havant on 1 September 1951 is headed by Class A1X 'Terrier' 0-6-0T No 32655. The Hayling Island line closed in the winter of 1963 and ironically not because the line itself was losing money. The Southern Region had to admit the route was profitable as even then it provided a far faster way off the Island compared with the single north-south road which even nearly sixty years ago was choked with traffic. Instead it was the condition of this bridge over the water that was the contention, the cost of replacement/repair simply could not be justified whilst modern diesel units were considered too heavy for the structure.

A1X class 'Terrier' 0-6-0T No 32661 hauls another Hayling Island train away from Havant on 1 September 1951. Due to its almost unique status the route thus became a mecca for the enthusiast especially in later years. Four coaches were also a substantial load for the railway and, as such, a lot was expected of the little engines that worked the line. Because of their diminutive size and limited bunker capacity, coal was available at both Havant and Hayling although it of course had to be hand shovelled (or even thrown) into the bunker!

'The East Anglian' express awaits departure from Liverpool Street on 11 March 1952, headed by BR 'Britannia' Pacific No 70002 *Geoffrey Chaucer*. The service had been inaugurated on 27 August 1937 and operated in either direction between Liverpool Street and Norwich Thorpe with one intermediate stop at Ipswich. As first introduced the train took 2¼ hours in either direction – reduced by five minutes each way the following year. A single set of six coaches were provided for the service replete with two restaurant cars, one for first class and one for third class. Excluding restaurant car seating the capacity was for 36 first and 120 third class passengers.

The 12.15pm (circular) Sunday service from Cannon Street to Charing Cross awaits departure on 7 October 1951, behind L1 class 4-4-0 No 31787. The class were a beautifully proportioned design and indeed had charge of several of the principal passenger workings on the South Eastern section until usurped by larger designs in the 1930s and subsequent electrification. Considered still to have some life remaining, a few were transferred to the Western Section in the early 1950s and then again from 1959 onwards. Unfortunately, by the latter date steam was already in decline and after some time at Nine Elms the end came for No 31787 in 1961.

'Jubilee' 4-6-0 No 45568 *Western Australia* hammers along the down fast line away from Elstree tunnel on 12 April 1952, heading 'The Thames-Clyde Express' from St Pancras to Glasgow St Enoch. These three-cylinder engines were built between 1934 and 1936 and could be seen on most areas of the former LMS system. Similar in appearance to the ubiquitous 'Black 5', two obvious differences were the protrusion over the front framing for the tail of the piston rod serving the middle cylinder and also the fact that a name was being carried. The engine is seen here attached to a small Midland tender but they could also be seen with a standard Stanier LMS tender, which aesthetically suited them well.

Passing east of Shenfield, where the electrification then ended, BR 'Britannia' Pacific No 70003 *John Bunyan* hauls a Liverpool Street-Norwich express on 10 May 1952. The 'Britannia' class revolutionised the former GE lines out of Liverpool Street in the 1950s before electrification, here at last was a modern steam locomotive that was reliable and had power to spare so enabling schedules to be cut, especially once away from the congested suburban area. Small wonder then the GE men took them to their hearts and whilst the Standard designs were sometimes regarded as giving a harsh ride and had dusty working conditions, they were nevertheless well liked. They were eventually replaced by diesel and eventually overheard electrification.

A Liverpool Street-Southend-on-Sea (Victoria) train passes Mountnessing Junction, east of Shenfield and Hutton, on 19 May 1952, headed by Holden Class B12/3 4-6-0 No 61572. The old order is represented here, and also typified by the variety of coaching stock seen. Unlike on today's modern railway where it is possible for the regular traveller to predict with almost 100% accuracy where the carriage doors will come to rest on the platform, decades ago it could be different on a daily basis, GER and LNER coaching stock comprising the working.

ABOVE Class B12/3 4-6-0 No 61546 comes under the Norwich main line again at Mountnessing Junction, this time on 10 May 1952 and whilst in charge of a Liverpool Street-Southend-on-Sea (Victoria) train. Today the B12 class is represented by just one example, that seen in the previous view, No 61572; the engine seen here coming to the end of its days in May 1959.

RIGHT Near Shanklin on 11 June 1952, Class O2 0-4-4T No W23 *Totland* steams freely with the 11.42am Isle of Wight service from Ventnor to Ryde Pier Head. Like the Hayling Island line a few miles east on the mainland, the lines on the Isle of Wight were another attraction typifying railways belonging to another age. Even so their isolation did not mean they were being ignored by headquarters at Waterloo and Marylebone had already made inroads into (or were about to) the Freshwater, Newport-Sandown, Ventnor West, and Bembridge lines. The O2 class though still had more than a decade to operate services and would continue on Ryde-Ventnor and Ryde-Cowes services until the end of 1966.

'The Master Cutler' express for Sheffield departs from Marylebone on 5 July 1952, powered by Class A3 Pacific No 60052 *Prince Palatine*. The train consist appears to comprise mainly brand new BR Mk1 stock painted in the attractive 'blood and custard' livery that was so redolent of the period. The engine itself was one of the numerous A3 class, several of which were named after famous racehorses from the 1930s. Of equal interest is the train on the left comprising of at least one ro-rail milk tanker and several other standard six-wheel milk tank cars.

Railfans gather on Platform 8 at King's Cross on 5 July 1952 to see A1 class Pacific No 60122 *Curlew* depart with the 'Aberdonian'. The A1 design were the final example of the 'Pacific' designs produced by the LNER with examples being built into BR days. Again three-cylinder engines, they were both popular and reliable even though at the time never quite catching the imagination of an 'A4'. That would change in later years whilst few could have grasped how the new-build steam locomotive *Tornado* would capture the imagination of the enthusiast and public alike especially since it has been the only recorded steam locomotive in recent years to have officially been allowed to reach 100mph.

Before the tracks were quadrupled, A3 Pacific No 60106 *Flying Fox* passes Hadley Wood at speed on 13 July 1952, powering the 10.00am Sunday express from King's Cross to Newcastle. The coaching stock is a mixture of late LNER and new build BR Mk1 stock, the latter coming into use on all regions and allocated to the prestige trains of the day. This in turn resulted in a cascade effect with relatively modern LNER vehicles appearing on secondary services far sooner than would otherwise have been the case.

Gangers stand aside as Class B1 4-6-0 No 61027 *Madoqua* emerges from Hadley North tunnel with a mixed freight from Peterborough to King's Cross goods on 13 July 1952. It is all too easy to forget the importance the men on the track contributed to the safe running of the railway. Few had any formal engineering training and yet they could judge by eye where repairs were required and 'fettle' the rails, ballast and sleepers to the exact amount required. A lookout would warn of the impending approach of a train and it was then time for a few moments relaxation before returning to what was often said to be the hardest task on the whole railway.

Portrait of an A4 at speed. No 60008 *Dwight D. Eisenhower* passes Hadley Wood at speed on 13 July 1952, powering 'The West Riding' express, but not carrying the appropriate headboard. As with the previous image the rolling stock is a mixture of types. Thirty-five of the A4 class were built but one was destroyed beyond economical repair during enemy action at York in WW2. No doubt it yielded some spares regardless. The remainder of the class survived intact until four were withdrawn at the end of 1962, their prestige role now usurped by diesel traction. No 60008 was destined to be one of the six survivors and spent its early preservation years in a museum in North America. It was repatriated, briefly, for 'The Great Gathering' held at the National Railway Museum in 2013 but was subsequently returned to its American museum.

The 12.18pm Sunday express from King's Cross to Newcastle passes under the North London Line viaduct that spans the East Coast main line at Belle Isle, between Gasworks and Copenhagen tunnels, on 13 July 1952, powered by A3 class Pacific No 60056 *Centenary;* this view taken from the steps of Belle Isle signal box. Aside from the seemingly almost endless procession of trains that passed this point both coming and going, the area will forever be associated with the wonderful 1955 Ealing comedy 'The Ladykillers'. In this a stellar cast of actors take rooms with an elderly lady to hide their intentions of robbing cash from a train at nearby King's Cross. Initially they succeed, only to be eventually thwarted and meet their end one by one, the last being hit on the head by a signal and falling into an empty wagon passing on a train below.

LEFT 'A4s' on freight were never a common sight, and when one did turn up, it somehow always looked incongruous. Before the station was renamed Alexandra Palace, No 60010 *Dominion of Canada* passes Wood Green on 19 September 1952, hauling fish vans from Aberdeen, most of the contents of which will eventually arrive at Billingsgate Market. Assuming the A4 to be in good mechanical condition this was a cost saving way of ensuring an engine from elsewhere could return to its home depot earning revenue at the same time. The legendary King's Cross driver Bill Hoole recounts working one of these trains with an A4 just after the crew had been made aware of a recent 100mph dash by a sister engine. Always keen on speed, Bill was quite prepared to have a go at equalling and even beating that figure, that is until he realised exactly what he had coupled behind the tender!

BELOW 2P 4-4-0 No 40672 on shed at Watford Junction on 9 August 1952. The former Midland Railway 2P class were broadly similar in outline to the compound design seen earlier, the principal difference being the lack of compounding and that these engines had inside cylinders. Clearly taken on a wet day, we may note the storm sheets rigged in the cab, better than nothing no doubt but the rain would probably have found some way in. Aside from work on the LMS main line, examples of the class were allocated to the Somerset & Dorset route and so could be seen as far south as Bournemouth.

A rare locomotive type to be seen on the Great Northern main line, Holden ex-Great Eastern Railway 'Claud Hamilton' D16/3 class 4-4-0 No 62618 emerges from Hadley North tunnel on 19 July 1952, rostered for a Cambridge-King's Cross semi-fast train. Rebuilt from a Belpaire-boilered Class D16/2, the engine still retains its original decorative valancing and was once the designated 'Royal Engine'. Inroads into the numbers in service were made throughout the 1950s, the engine seen here lasting until the winter of 1959 whilst the last survivor was taken out of service the following year. It had been hoped one of the type would have been retained for official preservation but this was not to be although a 'new build' is in the planning stage.

ABOVE Winding round the slow line cutting from Watford tunnel on 9 August 1952, Hughes 5MT 'Crab' No 42887 hauls a lengthy freight from its home base of (Manchester) Longsight (9A) to Willesden. The nickname 'Crab' came from the stepped framing and massive looking cylinders, slightly out of proportion perhaps when viewed from certain angles but this did not detract from what was a strong and popular engine, the last examples of which almost made it to the very end of steam on British Railways.

RIGHT BR Standard 4MT 2-6-4T No 80039 enters Watford cutting, north of the station, on 9 August 1952, hauling a semi-fast service from Euston to Bletchley. This design was one of the undoubted success stories of the 1950s with examples seen at work on most regions in the 1950s. Several were built at Brighton, a number of these remaining on the Southern Region where there was a distinct shortage of and, indeed, a dire need for a large tank engine. Notice the curving tank sides, deliberately engineered to ensure the engine was within specific load gauges and could therefore work with greater route availability. The oval buffers allowed for shunting on tight curves where ordinary round buffers might otherwise have locked together.

LEFT AVC Demonstration Rail Cars 1, 2 & 3, having arrived at Watford Junction as the 5.53pm local service from St Albans Abbey, prepare to return on 9 August 1952. The set undertook trial workings on a number of branch lines including the Allhallows-on-Sea line in Kent and between Didcot and Newbury, although in the latter case this was a trial run without passengers. Powered by two 125hp engines acceleration could be brisk but the ride could be rough on track that was not maintained to main line standards. Top speed was 50mph.

BELOW GWR AEC Railcar No W26 arrives at its Leamington Spa destination with its trailer coach on 25 August 1952, forming a local service from Stratford-upon-Avon. This is an interesting combination as whilst individually both the diesel railcar and the auto-coach could be worked from either end (the auto-coach of course needing a 14xx steam engine at the Guard's end), the make up here was not so compatible and if a return working were required, the railcar would have to run round. Perhaps there was a need for extra passenger accommodation at short notice or it was a means of working the coach forward rather than as a separate special working.

Between 4COR electric unit No 3149, forming a train to Portsmouth Harbour, and H16 class Pacific Tank No 30520 hauling empty coaching stock, Maunsell 'King Arthur' 4-6-0 No 30751 *Etarre* departs from Waterloo on 23 August 1952, with a train for Bournemouth West. It would not be long before sights such as this began to fade from memory as with the influx of BR Standard type tender engines, so the 'King Arthur' class would slowly be erased from the scene although they would continue to be employed on 'inter-regional' trains to and from the Southern Region. Lacking perhaps the charisma of a Pacific, the type was nevertheless solid and reliable and in consequence often preferred by the motive power department for their predictable performance.

Hauling a mixed rake of wagons towards Birmingham, 93xx Mogul No 9306 passes through Leamington Spa station on 25 August 1952. The position of the two lamps indicated to the signalman that this was a through freight and so not calling at intermediate stopping points, although it could well have been sidelined at times into loops or refuge sidings to allow a faster train to pass. Upon arrival at destination the service will be broken up into component parts perhaps as little as a single wagon, these being reformed again so traffic was correctly routed to its respective destinations. Unless needing to turn off the main line, the bell code between signal boxes for such a working was '1 pause 4'.

Oswestry (89A)-allocated 'Manor' 4-6-0 No 7819 *Hinton Manor* pulls away from Oswestry station on 28 August 1952, heading the 10.50am service to Pwllheli. The Manor class were the largest engines regularly allowed on to the former Cambrian lines and together with the smaller 4-4-0 'Dukedog' type formed the mainstay of motive power to both Pwllheli and Aberystwyth until supplemented by the BR Standard Class 4 '75xxx' during the final years of steam. Oswestry had for many years been the headquarters of the locomotive works for the former Cambrian company. Hard to imagine that almost everything seen here was swept away following closure in 1966. Fortunately the main buildings were listed Grade 2 and survive whilst No 7819 has been preserved and has been based on the Severn Valley Railway for many years.

Wolverhampton Stafford Road (84A)-allocated Star class 4-6-0 No 4049 *Princess Maud* awaits departure from Shrewsbury on 28 August 1952 with an express for Paddington. The 'Star' class were the first development of the Churchward four-cylinder 4-6-0 and were a revelation when the initial engines took to the rails in 1906. Later developments came with the 'Castle' and finally the 'King' class, each in turn cascading the 'Star' type on to lesser duties. No 4049 was thus slightly unusual as being seen on an express working at this time, perhaps she was regarded as a 'good un'. All were gone by the end of the 1950s although one, No 4003 *Lode Star*, survives as a non operational museum piece.

The 16.50 local service to Gobowen awaits departure from Shrewsbury on 28 August 1952, headed by Leamington Spa (84D)-allocated 'Saint' 4-6-0 No 2933 *Bibury Court*. The 'Saint' class were another GWR design dating back to the early years of the 20th century and from which spawned the 330 members of the 'Hall' class as well as the 'Grange' 'and 'Manor' classes. The 'Saint' type and its successors were all two- cylinder engines, but with the huge 6' 8½" driving wheels giving them a fair turn of speed when required. Unfortunately all of the original engines were eventually scrapped, but in 2019 the Great Western Society unveiled a magnificent new-build, *Lady of Legend*, using components from a former 'Hall' to effectively deconstruct the development and restore an original.

Still with GWR on the tank sides, 14xx class 0-4-2T No 1432 pulls away from Oswestry on 28 August 1952, heading the 11.20am auto train to Gobowen. This was a non-auto fitted working with the coaches too in different liveries: 'crimson and cream' and all over 'maroon'. Originally numbered No 4832, the 48xx series of numbers was given over to 'Hall' class engines converted to burn oil from 1946 onwards and although oil burning did not last long and the converts relinquished their revised numbering, the renumbering of the 0-4-2T design was to remain permanent.

At Shrewsbury on 28 August 1952, 'Hall' class 4-6-0 No 4976 *Warfield Hall* departs with a train of Southern coaching stock, forming a Hastings-Birkenhead inter-regional express, while Class 8F 2-8-0 No 48706 is signal checked in the centre road with a freight for Crewe, and in the shadow of the station canopy on the right is 'Saint' 4-6-0 No 2933 *Bibury Court*, awaiting departure with the 16.50 local service for Gobowen. The family resemblance from the 'Saint' is obvious with the 'Hall' whilst it might even be said that Sir William Stanier's 8F standing in the middle road was a similar development from the Saint as had not Stanier been trained at Swindon before leaving to take up the top job on the LMS? The signal bridge displays both three and four foot arms whilst two backing signals are also present.

Theoretically, it was possible to record a train coming over Battledown Viaduct at the same time as one passed beneath, but I did not manage to accomplish this until over 30 years later in 1984! Before this time and leaning to the curve, Urie H15 class 4-6-0 No 30487 clanks under the structure with another freight working, this one from Plymouth to Nine Elms. The H15 class were ideal for this type of work which they shared with the S15 design. Known as 'Chonkers', the H15 class were heavily built engines which would slog away with almost any load but could also burn an economical amount of coal in the process.

Another class 5MT 'Crab' type Mogul No 42870 passes the Bushey troughs water tower on 25 March 1953, heading a northbound freight. We had an example of a 'Crab' earlier, this one here perhaps having picked up water at the troughs although it would depend on the speed of the train – too slow and the forward momentum would be insufficient to lift the water from the scoop into the tender. Unfitted freight trains would spend much of their time travelling slowly and so water might more usually be taken at water columns strategically placed at the end of loops or refuge sidings – but then it was also a skill to bring the train to rest at exactly the right point so the arm of the water column would be in line with the tender filler.

Class B17/4 4-6-0 No 61648 *Arsenal* climbs Brentwood Bank on 9 May 1953, hauling the 8.45am service from Liverpool Street to Southend Central. Above the engine the electrified wires indicate the future for the line – and of course many others. In the 1950s and, certainly later, the 1960s, steam and everything associated with it was 'yesterdays' travel, lack of investment after nationalisation resulting in the railways having to struggle on with antiquated and outmoded equipment. Under continued private ownership there was no guarantee it would have been any better hence the closure programmes which started in the 1950s – Dr Beeching was really only the name who accelerated these closures – allied to attempts at standardisation with both locomotives and rolling stock along with more efficient working created through the introduction of more diesel and electric trains.

Travelling the connecting loop line between St Mary Cray Junction and Chislehurst on a spring-like 20 February 1953, Maunsell SE&CR N class Mogul No 31404 hauls loaded wooden-sided coal wagons from Betteshanger Colliery towards London. There are still those who find it hard to believe Kent was once a coal producing area but the north-east corner was rich in coal and generated much traffic for the railway. Even so, the largest freight engines on the former South Eastern lines were generally the N type, supplemented by the Q1 design when required.

ABOVE Hauling southbound coal wagons from Stourbridge Junction on 11 April 1953, Class 43xx Mogul No 4375 passes between Denham and West Ruislip. We also see a mixture of wooden and later build mineral wagons, the former very likely former private owner wagons taken into the general wagon pool in the 1940s. Some would also have grease axleboxes meaning frequent stops were necessary to refill with grease. If one of these were to run 'hot' the result could be drops of flaming grease and 'seven bells' to the next signal box ahead, meaning 'stop and examine'.

RIGHT A K3 Mogul was uncommon motive power for Liverpool Street-Southend-on-Sea passenger traffic, but nevertheless No 61835 was brought into use for such a working on 9 May 1953, and is shown here pounding up the 1 in 85 of Brentwood Bank towards Ingrave summit. The origins of the type were as the Great Northern H4 design with further batches completed until there were a total of 193 in existence in 1937. The engines secured the nickname 'Jazzers' due to the rhythm of their exhaust and unbalanced movement caused by the three-cylinder design. One was later rebuilt with just two cylinders and given the designation K5 but no further rebuilds followed. With the demise of steam all were scrapped but again there are long term plans for a 'new-build' K3.

Allocated to Dover shed (74C), Schools class 4-4-0 No 30921 *Shrewsbury* climbs Hildenborough Bank on 23 May 1953 with an express from Dover Marine to London. When Bulleid fitted a multiple jet blastpipe and larger chimney to some half of the class in 1938, the performance of the locomotives certainly improved - but not necessarily their appearance. The Schools type were without doubt the finest 4-4-0s ever built but despite the limited wheel arrangement they were not the last; that distinction falling to the GWR with their Bulldog/Duke conversions of the 1930s in the form of the Dukedog type. Of the Schools, a few had gone before but the vast majority were condemned with the stroke of a pen on that fateful day 30 December 1962 which saw the end of over a hundred Southern engines, many in good condition with potentially years of useful life left. *Shrewsbury* was not to be one of the survivors and was recycled by the scrapyard of Messrs Cohens at Kettering.

Hauling a heavy holiday relief for Cannon Street, Wainwright SE&CR L class 4-4-0 No 31771 struggles up the 1 in 122 gradient of Hildenborough Bank on 23 May 1953. When photographed, the train was travelling at no more than 5mph, and it seemed that the 1914-built locomotive would stall at any minute – but its manful struggles paid off and it managed to reach the summit at Sevenoaks Tunnel, after which it recovered on the downhill 1 in 160 stretch of line to Dunton Green. Today's trains make short work of gradients such as these but in steam days a lot depended on the condition of the engine, the type of coal, the crew and the rail conditions. From the exhaust it looks like the fireman is doing his best, the driver has the engine probably in full-forward gear and hopefully it was a dry day. To stall under such conditions would mean a walk to the signal box in rear to arrange for assistance and all the delays such a move would entail.

ABOVE With ample steam to spare, Britannia Pacific No 70004 *William Shakespeare* descends Hildenborough Bank at speed on 23 May 1953, heading the 'Golden Arrow' express from London Victoria to Dover Marine. A different example of steam to that seen previously, little apparent effort and with steam to spare. In the early 1950s, No 70004 always shone a little more than her sisters which was due to the exhibition finish of her paintwork as a result of display at the 1951 'Festival of Britain' exhibition on the south bank of the Thames. Sadly she would end her days unkempt and was withdrawn after just sixteen years' service and scrapped in 1968.

RIGHT 61xx class Prairie tank No 6103 approaches High Wycombe with a local service from Banbury on 6 June 1953. The Great Western and later BR Western Region had a number of the 51xx and 61xx types for suburban local working and with the 61xx type seen mainly in the London and Birmingham areas of the former GWR system. One lamp under the chimney signified a stopping passenger service – not as on the Southern the route to be taken. Notice in the 'four-foot' between the rails an ATC ramp which will be sounding a siren in the cab of the engine as the associated distant signal is 'on'. The distant signal is also motor operated from the next signal box ahead. Finally, note a spare ATC ramp lies on its side parallel with the rails.

ABOVE N2/2 class 0-6-2T No 69542 emerges from Copenhagen Tunnel and begins the climb of Holloway Bank towards Finsbury Park on 29 June 1953, hauling the 10.00am local service from King's Cross to Hertford North. This engine is fitted with condensing pipes for working on the 'Widened Lines' underground. Intended to condense the exhaust steam within the water of the side tanks and so not only reduce steam emission but also save water, it was something also practised on certain GWR and LMS engine types. Success was marginal whilst as here a condensing engine could also be seen working a conventional, surface train.

LEFT King's Cross (34A)-based A4 Pacific No 60003 *Andrew K. McCosh* blasts away from Copenhagen Tunnel on 29 June 1953 and starts the climb of Holloway Bank with 'The Norseman' express from King's Cross to Newcastle Tyne Commission Quay, carrying passengers for Norway. Having a lineside pass was essential to obtain images such as this. 'At your own risk' was the wording but they were freely available and probably hundreds took advantage of the opportunity. The ground would shake as a train such as this went past – you just had to hope no-one chose that moment to throw something out of a window!

ABOVE Unusually working a Peterborough-King's Cross semi-fast service, New England (35A)-allocated Class A2 Pacific No 60533 *Happy Knight* drifts down Holloway Bank towards Copenhagen Tunnel on 29 June 1953. A main line express engine working a semi-fast turn could happen for several reasons. It may have been a normal part of the diagram, the engine might have worked an 'extra' and this was the easiest way of returning it to its home depot, it may have developed a fault, been repaired and again was being returned, or perhaps the more likely from the image of the poor external condition of the engine, it may be awaiting a repair and for the present at least is being used restricted to other than on front-line turns.

LEFT A1 class Pacific No 60156 *Great Central* powers away from Copenhagen Tunnel on 29 June 1953, hauling the northbound 'Flying Scotsman' express, unusually at this time complete with headboard. The engine name commemorates the former LNER constituent company, other members of the class recalling the 'North British', 'Great Eastern', and 'North Eastern' concerns. No 60156 was one of twenty-four of the class that ceased working in 1965, redundant due to dieselisation but also affected by lack of maintenance. At the time none were preserved (although unsuccessful efforts had been made to secure No 60145), hence the interest in the new-build *Tornado* which has carved a deserved name for itself since emerging in 2008.

Breaking from the sulphurous, smoky atmosphere of Copenhagen Tunnel on 4 July 1953, Class A2/3 Pacific No 60520 *Owen Tudor* comes to terms with the 1 in 100 gradient of Holloway Bank with a King's Cross-Harrogate express. On the ground to the left of the engine is a wooden fogmans hut and also a concrete latrine. It is also just possible to discern a hand lever and rod going towards the rail. In poor weather a fogman would be stationed here whose job was to place a detonator on the track if the distant signal displayed 'caution' – unlike that seen here on this occasion. The fogman's role was an essential if lonely and cold task with little comfort other than a brazier in which to burn coal to keep warm even if the resultant smoke added to the general murk all round.

B2 4-6-0 No 61615 *Culford Hall* departs from London Liverpool Street on 7 July 1953, heading the 12.36pm 'Clacton Interval Service'. The Great Western were thus not the only railway company to have 'Hall' class engines although to be fair at 330 engines they did have slightly more than the LNER! Again the overhead wires are visible so the fireman would ensure he would not be using any of the long fire irons in the vicinity. Perhaps it is surprising the later red/white electrification 'warning flash' danger signs were not introduced earlier.

Gresley 'A4' Pacific No 60017 *Silver Fox* blasts out of Copenhagen Tunnel on the climb away from King's Cross on 11 July 1953 with the northbound 'Elizabethan' express for Edinburgh Waverley. The tunnels immediately out of King's Cross were a trial for many heavy trains. Hard to relate but a steam engine needs to warm through to give of its best; steam passages, cylinders, pistons and valves all need to reach an optimum temperature and this would take some miles to achieve. Hence long distance and heavy trains were often banked (given a shove) the length of the platform at King's Cross (and indeed at other termini as well) by which point at King's Cross at least the train engine would be well into the tunnel and so alone in charge of the train.

Framed in Gasworks Tunnel, New England (35A)-allocated Class V2 2-6-2 No 60966 powers the 9.00am boat train from King's Cross to Newcastle Tyne Commission Quay on 11 July 1953. 'The Norseman' was one of the fastest post-war expresses on the East Coast Main Line and ran exclusively for passengers bound for Norway on Wednesdays and Saturdays only, during three months of the summer timetable. In the early 1950s, several members of the V2 class were loaned to the Southern Region consequent upon axle problems with the 'Merchant Navy' class. The visitors acquainted themselves well, some crews reported as sad to see them return to the Eastern Region.

Climbing away from Copenhagen Tunnel on 11 July 1953, Gresley 'A4' No 60003 *Andrew K. McCosh* heads north from King's Cross with the 9.40am 'Norwegian Express' for Newcastle Tyne Commission Quay. Without a headboard it was not always easy to identify a specific train whilst to the signalman such workings would all be 'four beats' meaning express passenger. Here was where the working timetable came into its own for a good signalman would (should) always know what was expected next and if out of course working was in place he would rely upon the signal box in rear or control to advise as to what the train approaching actually was.

Gresley V2 class 2-6-2 No 60877 blasts away from Copenhagen Tunnel on 11 July 1953, and begins the climb to Finsbury Park with an express from King's Cross to Hull. The V2 class were potentially the most versatile of all the large Gresley types. Equally at home on all but the heaviest and fastest turns, these were the engines that were recorded as hauling trains in excess of twenty coaches in WW2 and were even dubbed 'the engines that won the war' although the same accolade could be similarly applied to many other types. At the end of their lives a few found their way to Swindon, unfortunately not for work but where their tenders were instead modified for further use, the engines themselves being of little value and scrapped.

D34 class 4-4-0 No 62490 *Glen Fintaig* arrives at Edinburgh Waverley on 25 July 1953, with a local service from North Berwick. Built to the design of 'Willie' Reid for the North British Railway in 1920, this was one of a class of engines all named after Scottish lochs. Withdrawals started even before nationalisation with the first example going in 1946 and the last in 1961. One is preserved, No 256 *Glen Douglas*. In operational service they remained in Scotland on such duties as perishable turns, fish for example, from locations like Mallaig and Aberdeen as well as seen here on more humble local workings. Nameplates were not fitted, the name instead being painted on to the splasher.

Leaning to the curve, Pickersgill 3P 4-4-0 No 54466 is between Culloden Moor and Inverness with the 2.48pm train from Aviemore to the Highland capital. Super-elevation to the running rails is something applied to many main lines. It of course enables a more comfortable and if appropriate faster ride although we may doubt exactly how fast No 54466 was travelling. Preparing an inside cylinder engine such as this for duty would entail the driver oiling the links and pins of the valves and pistons between the frames, certainly not an easy task under certain conditions and at other times of the day. Such fittings would also need to be checked and replenished with oil at the end of each journey.

ABOVE The 17.15 sleeping car train from Inverness to London Euston nears Culloden Moor on 27 July 1953, powered by double-headed 'Black 5' 4-6-0s Nos 44979 and 44698. Double-heading was not the most economical way of working but again it was sometimes resorted to due to the weight of the train being over the prescribed limit for the section of line. It was advisable for the crew on the second engine to keep their heads inside the cab as lumps of coal could become dislodged from the leading engine especially where the track might be a bit rough.

RIGHT Drummond Highland Railway 'Small Ben' 2P 4-4-0 No 54398 *Ben Alder* was one of twenty of the class built just before the turn of the century and was one of only three to receive a British Railways number in 1948. On 26 July 1953, it was a surprise 'find' in the Cairngorm Works yard in Inverness as it had been withdrawn months earlier. I later learnt that it was scheduled for preservation, but in fact it was later broken up, some say by accident, others by design.

The 10.52am train to Keith awaits departure from Forres on 29 July 1953, behind ex-Caledonian '920' class 3P 4-4-0 No 54471. The engine is showing clear signs of previous hard work in the form of the burnt patch at the base of the smokebox door. This was caused by a build up of burning ash and char at the same point on the inside of the smokebox and which could sometimes even reach beyond the dart handles. Cleaning the smokebox was then a case of pot luck; the whole lot could come down on the feet of the unfortunate fireman or shed labourer once the door was opened or it might have remained as a solid perhaps even red hot mass, needing to be emptied rather more carefully.

RIGHT 'Black 5' 4-6-0 No 44980 awaits departure from Aberdeen on 29 July 1953, with 'The Granite City' express. The use of a 'Black 5' on this working displays the versatility of the class, able to work both passenger and freight turns. This train operated in both directions between Aberdeen and Glasgow and had first been inaugurated in 1933. It was curtailed in 1939 but reintroduced again post-1948.

BELOW Holden 1911 Great Eastern B12/1 4-6-0 No 61502 departs from Aberdeen on 29 July 1953 with the 6.10pm service to Keith. This was an engine now far away from its original home on the Great Eastern lines out of Liverpool Street. Some members of the class were indeed cascaded elsewhere following their routing from East Anglia although it was to be a short lived life extension as all had gone by 1961.

ABOVE BR Standard 4MT 2-6-4T No 80004 makes a spirited departure from Aberdeen on 29 July 1953, powering the 6.33pm local service to Fraserburgh. As modern replacements for engines going back thirty-plus years the BR Standard tank design was almost universally welcomed. Fast, powerful and economical on fuel, they were also comfortable to work on but could be prone to roll slightly at speed. Examples would last to the end of steam in 1968 and several have been preserved.

RIGHT Ex-Great Eastern Railway F4 class 2-4-2T No 67157 inside Kittybrewster shed (61A), Aberdeen, on 30 July 1953. Engines of this type were purloined during WW2 to work mobile anti-aircraft services on several parts of the system ranging from the East Coast, Scotland and as far away as the South-West. Some were fitted with armour plating whilst an experiment at the same time was a fitment of 'armoured plastic' which under certain trial conditions proved more resilient than steel. Unfortunately the distances needing to be run to reach their new areas of work in WW2 was not contusive to thirty year old bearings and a number arrived at their new (temporary as it turned out) homes requiring attention to wheel bearings and axle boxes.

ABOVE Epping shed on 8 August 1953 with J15 class 0-6-0s 65444 & 65449 and C12 4-4-2 Tank No 67363. Here was an example of steam suburban working from just a couple of generations past. At the time all of the engines seen were survivors from pre-grouping days and yet they remained, fulfilling a useful service. The missing brickwork from the front of what is otherwise a modern steam depot may well be a leftover from WW2.

TOP RIGHT Super power for three motley coaches. Class B12/3 4-6-0s Nos 61569 & 61571 lay a blanket of smoke over Cambridge on 19 August 1953 as they depart with the 11.17am service for Ipswich. Possibly another example of returning an engine to its home depot other than as a light engine working but certainly not an economical use of motive power. It also shows how some B12s remained on their home turf. At least five working railwaymen would be on the train, the two crews from the engines and a guard. The middle coach is also the most antiquated and appears to be a former GE clerestory.

BOTTOM RIGHT Class B17/6 'Footballer' No 61655 *Middlesbrough* climbs Brentwood Bank and heads for Ingrave Summit on 5 September 1953, hauling an express from Liverpool Street to Clacton-on-Sea. Pristine condition indicates perhaps a recent works visit although some depots were also better at cleaning than others. Some twenty-five members of the type were named after football clubs, most if not all also having a brass football as part of the nameplate. Not surprisingly such items are now much sought after in collectors' sales.

Ex-Johnson Midland Railway 1P 0-4-4T No 58038 approaches Romford on 5 September 1952, with the 12.14 shuttle from Upminster. This is another example of the class seen earlier on the same type of working. The rolling stock is non-corridor and evidently a warm day from the number of droplights in the open position. Notice the faded 'British Railways' working on the tank sides, an early method of designating nationalised ownership prior to the introduction of the 'cycling lion' emblem.

Having been derailed following a collision outside Stratford 'New Shed' on 5 September 1953, Class J69/2 0-6-0T No 68510 is crane-lifted back on to the tracks. Damage was minimal and the loco remained in service at 30A until 1959. Most of the major locomotive sheds had a breakdown crane and gang ready to attend similar instances, the men of the gang having their normal duty; a fitter, boiler maker, etc, as well as having the stand-by task as a member of the gang. National working conditions also ensured that a breakdown allowance was paid should the crane or breakdown vans attend an incident outside of the shed precincts. Considering the close location of this incident to Stratford shed it is unlikely any such additional gratuity was paid.

ABOVE Climbing Holloway Bank towards Finsbury Park on 20 September 1953, Class C2 and C1 Atlantics No 990 *Henry Oakley* and No 251 power the 'Plant Centenarian' from King's Cross to Doncaster as part of the Doncaster Works centenary celebrations. The celebrations of 1953 were an excellent display of public relations by the Eastern Region but hard work for the engines as No 251 steamed badly having had its superheater removed and the size of the boiler flue tubes had not been adjusted to suit. Both engines remain in preserved state but are no longer operational.

RIGHT A4 Pacific No 60014 *Silver Link* blasts away from King's Cross on 27 September 1953, and passes under the North London Line at Belle Isle, with the northbound 'Plant Centenarian', celebrating the centenary of Doncaster Works for the second week, the trains working in opposite directions. Notice the burnished and quartered buffers, again specially fitted (and kept in store for such occasions).

ABOVE At Palace Gates station on 10 April 1954, class F5 2-4-2T No 67209 awaits departure with a service for North Woolwich. LNER and later Eastern Region suburban services were often identified by means of a destination board across the front of the locomotive. Although busy during peak hours, off-peak trains such as this were less well patronised and it may even be awaiting time before departing – with few delays from boarding and departing passengers, good timekeeping was easily achieved.

RIGHT (Peterborough) New England (35A)-based WD class 2-8-0 No 90428 trundles out of the southern end of Welwyn North tunnel on 17 April 1954, hauling a fitted freight from Peterborough to Hornsey yard. Note the construction year 1850 above the portal. Being a fitted train (meaning the continuous brake was available throughout operated from the engine) the schedule allowed for the service to maintain a faster speed compared with an unfitted freight. Even so with short-wheelbase 4-coupled vehicles in tow it was still nothing like the progress a passenger train might make. In the cab spectacle plate the face of the driver can clearly be seen.

RIGHT The 5.52pm train from King's Cross was always double-headed in its day as it travelled to both Cambridge and to Abbots Ripton, dividing at Hitchin. Motive power was usually a pair of Thompson 'B1' 4-6-0s or a 'B1' and a 'Sandringham'. On 11 May 1954, the leading Class B1 was No 61095 carrying a self-weighing tender and the 'B17/6' was No 61627 *Aske Hall*. Self-weighing tenders were an occasional attachment to a locomotive class and for the obvious reason of checking fuel consumption. It also saved the otherwise laborious process of counting weighted bags of coal at the start and end of each journey. Compatibility issues meant the tender design itself had to be suited with the locomotive class as well. On a test run, not only would the fuel used thus be able to be measured but the remaining firebox ashes/ clinker and smokebox ash also had to be weighed before an assessment of actual fuel consumption could be made. On this occasion there is no indication whether a trial was taking place.

BELOW Lined up outside King's Cross shed (34A) on 9 May 1954 are Classes A1 Pacific No 60155 *Borderer*, V2 2-6-2 No 60903 and A4 Pacific No 60034 *Lord Faringdon*. No 60034 shows the method of gaining access to the smokebox of the A4 although in this view the bottom half of the sloping plate has not been dropped to the horizontal. This latter part afforded a step for the fireman/shedman from which the smokebox could be cleaned.

LEFT Carrying an inverted headboard marked 'Grantham', Class A4 Pacific No 60014 *Silver Link* descends Holloway Bank towards Copenhagen Tunnel on 11 April 1954, with the un-named 8.35am express from Glasgow to King's Cross. The inverted headboard likely meant the actual item was simply being transported back to its home depot. Most named services had more than a single headboard available for the simple expediency if one should be left at the wrong end of the journey or not transferred between locomotives.

Passing under the Caledonian Road bridge on 11 May 1954, a King's Cross bound 'Cambridge Buffet Express' drifts down the incline towards Copenhagen Tunnel, headed by the Royal Engine of the day, Class B2 4-6-0 No 61671 *Royal Sovereign*. This engine was kept in as good a condition as possible being used on Royal Workings when HM was travelling to and from the Sandringham estate. Even so it had to earn its keep on other occasions!

Approaching Brentwood at Ingrave summit on 30 June 1954, BR Standard 7MT 'Britannia' Pacific No 70036 *Boadicea* powers an express for Liverpool Street that had emanated from Cromer and Sheringham. Again signs of progress for the future are apparent with the overhead wires and colour light signals – the latter of an early type. *Boadicea* is fitted with the original arrangement of handrails on the smoke deflectors, most of the class later having a revised arrangement of hand holds cut into the metal to increase visibility ahead. This came about following the accident at Milton (Didcot) the following year when it was suggested the driver's view ahead may have been compromised by the presence of the original handrails.

On the higher reaches of Brentwood Bank, Holden Class B12/3 4-6-0 No 61549 has a very easy task heading in the direction of London on 30 June 1954 with just two vans. This locomotive was one of about twelve of the fleet to be selected for use on ambulance trains for the American armed forces during WW2, the design's high route availability and light weight being ideally suited for travelling on routes and lines all over the country. Again we see an early type of colour light signal but with the modern addition of 'feathers' to indicate a route divergence. A lightweight train such as this could hardly have contributed much towards its own running costs let alone contributed towards the railway as a whole.

M7 class 0-4-4T No 30479 departs from Southampton Central on 2 July 1954, with a local service for Fawley. The train would follow the main line as far as Totton before turning south through Marchwood and Hythe to reach its destination. Passenger traffic was never heavy on the line with petroleum products from the coastal refinery at Fawley the greatest traffic. There was also and indeed still is movement of stores to and from the military port at Marchwood.

LMS Co-Co Diesel Electric No 10000 near Eastleigh on 2 July 1954, powering the down 'Royal Wessex' express. All five of the BR main-line diesels (excluding the 'Fell' machine) were concentrated on the SR in the early 1950s, this notwithstanding the 140 Bullied pacifics and members of the Britannia class that were also on the SR at the time. The diesel concentration was deliberate and intended so an indication of a concentrated diesel operation could be gauged. All five were later transferred to the LMR for similar operation. In the background a new signal bridge is in the process of being brought into service whilst to the right, but out of view, were the Eastleigh running sheds.

Another view of the double-headed 5.52pm King's Cross-Cambridge/Abbots Ripton. This time, on 7 July 1954, power was provided by a brace of B1s, Nos 61113 and 61233.

31xx class 2-6-2T No 3102 leaves the yards north of Wolverhampton on 20 July 1954, with a pick-up freight. Wolverhampton was very much an interchange point between the WR and LMR, each region also having its own station – a throwback to pre-nationalisation days. The 31xx class were one of the earlier designs of 2-6-2T on the WR and could often be seen on freight or banking duties, the latter through the Severn Tunnel or around Brimscombe in the Golden Valley near Stroud (Gloucs.).

Having arrived at the WR station at Wolverhampton 'Low Level' with 'The Inter-City' express from Paddington on 20 July 1954, 'King' 4-6-0 No 6000 *King George V* is turned on the Stafford Road (84A) turntable in order to make the return journey. This was a typical (G)WR manual turntable without the assistance of vacuum thus meaning the engine had to be balanced correctly in order for it to be turned.

'Manor' class 4-6-0 No 7827 *Lydham Manor* approaches Shrewsbury on 22 July 1954, hauling a long mixed freight from Chester. In this area the 78xx class were often to be seen working the principal passenger services from Shrewsbury over the Cambrian Coast lines, a duty they shared for many years with the 4-4-0 'Dukedogs', that is until the latter were ousted with an influx of BR Standard Class 4 engines in the 75xxx series.

1908 Beyer, Peacock built Cambrian Railways 0-6-0 No 895 arrives at Oswestry on 22 July 1954, with the 1.25pm local service from Gobowen. Here really was a survivor from another age but one which had also almost reached the end of its life for it was withdrawn from service just three months later. Notice how Swindon had also adapted the engine over the years with a standard GWR design boiler and fittings.

Shafts of sunlight strike through the roof of Gateshead shed (52A) on 26 August 1954, as the residents, Gresley V2 2-6-2 No 60868 and Worsdell G5 0-4-4Ts Nos 67257 & 67259, await their next turn of duty.

Class A8 pacific tank No 69891 departs from Darlington Bank Top on 28 August 1954, hauling a stopping service for Saltburn. These engines were a Gresley rebuild of the 1913 Raven fleet of 4-4-4Ts. The height of the bunker and low framing gives a particularly massive appearance to the rebuilding and as such a 'top-heavy' appearance. It could well be that they also rolled when travelling at speed.

ABOVE Making an attempt to black-out Doncaster, Class B17/1 'Sandringham' 4-6-0 No 61643 *Champion Lodge* departs from the station on 31 August 1954 with the 9.07am semi-fast train for Peterborough. The Eastern Region practice of painting the class number on the buffer beam can also be seen.

RIGHT A southbound mixed freight passes Doncaster MPD on 31 August 1954, hauled by Class B16/2 4-6-0 No 61421. The loco was one of seven original Raven North Eastern Railway 'B16/1s' rebuilt by Gresley with double Walschaerts gear and derived inside cylinder motion. Multi-cylinder engines (meaning those having either three or four cylinders) were easier on the track but more expensive both to build and maintain. In addition the driver would be required to attend to any number of additional oiling points within the frames. Here a somewhat travel weary engine has pulled up alongside the water column and may well be waiting for the signal to clear before being able to proceed further.

ABOVE The Swiss-built Brown Boveri gas-turbine No 18000 outside Swindon Works on 31 October 1954. The loco was powered by four independently mounted motors with spring drive, giving a rated horse-power of 2,500 and weighing 115tons. First introduced in 1950, it eventually went abroad after spending the greater part of its initial years undergoing various tests, modifications and repairs.

LEFT Inside a decidedly untidy Brighton Works on 2 October 1954, H2 class Brighton Atlantic No 32421 *South Foreland* receives a heavy overhaul. The two Atlantic classes operating on the Southern, both former LBSCR designs, owed their origins to the engines with a similar wheel arrangement on the Great Northern. Like their counterparts north of the Thames the 1950s would be their final decade of service, so this could also be the last works visit for the engine. All would be gone within a few years although on the Bluebell Railway a new-build project is well underway with a hoped for completion date of 2021.

ABOVE On specially laid 1' 11½" gauge tracks, Vale of Rheidol 2-6-2T No 7 (later to carry the name *Owain Glyndŵr)* in course of overhaul in Swindon Works on 24 April 1955. The loco was a Davies & Metcalfe design of 1902 and is still in use on the Vale of Rheidol line today.

RIGHT Making an impressive sight emerging from Copenhagen Tunnel and beginning the climb of Holloway Bank, Class A3 Pacific No 60063 *Isinglass* works a King's Cross to Peterborough semi-fast service on 8 May 1955. Apart from the single lamp under the chimney one could be forgiven for thinking this was an express working especially as the make up is of the modern Mk1 stock. Semi-fast services though were as much of the scene as everything else, the engines of the A3 class well capable of this type of duty.

ABOVE B4 0-4-0T No 30086 alongside Q1 0-6-0 No 33025 at Guildford shed (70C) in July 1955. Guildford shed was a rare semi-roundhouse on the former South Western lines and survived as a steam shed until the very end of steam working on the Southern Region in July 1967. There was little physical room for locomotive requirements in the area and consequently the shed was hemmed into a corner on the south-west corner of the site. The whole area formerly occupied is now a multi-storey car park.

LEFT J50/3 class 0-6-0T No 68983 emerges from the gloom of Copenhagen Tunnel into the spring sunshine on 30 April 1955, hauling empty coaching stock to Finsbury Park carriage sidings. Here also we have another view of the single lever detonator placing equipment. Two buckets, presumably of coal, also stand nearby – perhaps more was purloined from a passing engine when required!

ABOVE A Maidstone East to London Victoria train passes Bickley Junction on 27 July 1955, formed of 2HAL stock with No 2657 leading. The initials HAL were an abbreviation for 'half lavatory' and meaning one of the two vehicles making up each set was so provided. Most Southern units were electrically compatible and so different length trains could be combined according to traffic requirements and available platform lengths.

LEFT Climbing between Bickley and Bickley Junction on 27 July 1955, Battle of Britain Pacific No 34067 *Tangmere* powers the 'Kentish Belle' Pullman from London Victoria to Margate and Ramsgate. The name 'Thanet Belle' had originally been given to this train from when it was introduced in 1948 until 1951. In that year three cars were detached at Faversham and ran separately through to Canterbury East and in consequence the name was changed to that seen here. Unfortunately the Canterbury service was not profitable and it was withdrawn after just one year. The revised name was retained until the service was discontinued in 1958 in view of the pending completion of Phase One of the Kent Coast Electrification the following year. There would be no Pullman replacement with the new electric trains.

Waiting in expectation of the next 'cop', 'Spotters Bridge' at Crewe is well occupied on 20 August 1955, as Ivatt Class 2MT 2-6-2T No 41229 awaits departure from the bay platform in use with the 12.52pm local service to Northwich. I wonder if any reader might recognise himself from 55 years ago? Rebuilding is also in progress with a modern canopy being erected in the distance. Whilst it may have become popular in recent years to deride the term 'train-spotter', it should be remembered that there was little else for young boys (and sometimes girls) to do in the 1950s and this was a harmless and even educational pastime – many spotters learnt their UK geography by plotting where trains and engines had come from. At its peak the Ian Allan spotters club had in the order of 230,000 members and there were probably at least a similar number outside the organisation. Hence the boards at main stations advising what spotters could and could not do and exactly where they could stand so as to be out of the way.

Fitted with a Lemaitre exhaust, Bricklayers Arms-allocated Schools class 4-4-0 No 30938 *St. Olave's* emerges from Priory Tunnel on 24 September 1955 and prepares to stop at Dover Priory station on its first leg to London with a special relief from Dover. Whether the wide chimney did much to enhance the appearance of these engines is open to debate but it cannot be denied the change made an already good engine even better. Notice the initials 'SPL' on the lower route disc so indicating this was indeed an additional working.

ABOVE After nearly 50 years in service, Churchward 1906 designed 44xx class 2-6-2T No 4406 has probably its last photograph taken inside Swindon Works Cutting-up Shop on 5 November 1955. Some parts have already been removed, the buffers for example appear to have been unbolted, perhaps taken away for re-use. Similarly the coupling rods, pistons and valves may be recycled on to another engine. The whole gives the impression of 'dismantling' rather than 'cutting'. Evidently smokebox numberplates were not as highly prized as they are today.

RIGHT Specially restored to original condition with livery, number and name now all present for the occasion, London Tilbury & Southend Railway 3P 4-4-2T No 80 *Thundersley* passes Stratford on 11 March 1956, with the RCTS 'Southend Centenary Special'. This service ran from Bishopsgate Goods to Shoeburyness via Bethnal Green, Stratford, Forest Gate, Barking, Rainham, Tilbury Town, Pitsea, and Southend Central. The return followed the same route as far as Pitsea before going via Laindon, Barking, West Ham, and Gas Factory Junction to terminate at Fenchurch Street.

ABOVE LT electric loco No 2 *Thomas Lord* arrives at New Cross Gate on 3 June 1956, with an RCTS East London Line charter. Sister (or should that be 'brother'?) engine No 14 *Benjamin Disraeli* is attached to the rear. The name Thomas Lord relates to the man who provided for the cricket ground named after him; a public house in the village of West Meon in Hampshire is also named after him.

RIGHT Rebuilt only a few months previously, Merchant Navy Pacific No 35013 *Blue Funnel* receives attention in Eastleigh Works on 25 July 1956. With the driving wheels missing it is possible attention was needed to the axleboxes or inside motion, access to the latter far easier if the wheels were removed. The rebuilt Bulleid engines were styled very much along the lines of the BR Standard pacific types with a high running plate giving access to the motion. Removal of the air-smooth casing, which in reality did little to assist in lifting steam clear of the cab, also meant easier access to the boiler mountings.

ABOVE The 5.04pm local service for Llangollen awaits departure from Ruabon on 9 August 1956, headed by Class 51xx Prairie No 5103. From the water gushing from the injector overflow the fireman is in the process of refilling the boiler but has not quite got the balance right between the steam and water cocks. The two trolleys laden with parcels and baskets were a common sight for decades on station platforms but is something that has totally disappeared in recent years with parcels traffic no longer handled by today's railway.

LEFT The 15.45 local service from Wrexham to Bala near Ruabon on 9 August 1956, headed by Croes Newydd (84J)-based 58xx class 0-4-2T No 5810. This was a non-auto fitted version of the 14xx series of similar tank engines. Despite their diminutive appearance they had a surprising turn of speed and one was recorded at no less than 70mph in service.

ABOVE Hall 4-6-0 No 7911 *Lady Margaret Hall* and BR Caprotti 5MT 4-6-0 No 73125 at Shrewsbury on 13 August 1956, heading a Margate-Birkenhead express and a Cardiff-Manchester London Road service, respectively. Both engines are variations on the basic Hall and Class 5 design, No 7911 having a number of modifications, the visible ones being the plate frame bogie and flat sided Hawksworth tender. No 73125 has nothing obvious from the front but was one of a number of the class fitted with Caprotti rather than Walschearts valve gear, the purpose of which was to provide for more accurate valve movement and consequently more efficient use of steam.

LEFT After closure of the 2' 6" gauge Welshpool & Llanfair Railway (W&LR) in 1956, its two Beyer, Peacock 1902-built 0-6-0Ts Nos 822 and 823 were stored under cover inside Oswestry Works, hopefully awaiting preservation, and where No 823 was recorded here on 10 August 1956. Fortunately both engines were indeed saved and can now be found returned to their original haunts on the surviving section of the W & L.

Entering Bromley-by-Bow station on 4 May 1957, Stanier 4MT 2-6-4T No 42533 heads a local service from Fenchurch Street to Southend Central. The engine is in clean external condition and so may have recently returned from overhaul. Elsewhere modern flats stand alongside the line although most of the railway infrastructure is clearly from years past.

RIGHT Rebuilt Merchant Navy Pacific No 35012 *United States Line* passes Vauxhall on 4 May 1957, powering the down 'Atlantic Coast Express'. The engine still retains the small BR emblem on the tender which visually did not match the expanse of space on which it was placed. Notwithstanding the rebuilding applied, the Bulleid wheels, boiler, firebox, outside cylinders, smokebox door and cab have been retained. This engine was a hoped for preservation candidate and could well have followed No 60008 *Dwight D. Eisenhower* to preservation in North America. Sadly it seems BR forgot the hint that had been dropped by the Americans a few years earlier and she ended her days in appalling mechanical and external condition before being reduced to scrap.

BELOW The 5.02pm train to Dartford, via Sidcup, departs from Cannon Street on 6 May 1957, 2EPB No 5772 leading two four-car EPB sets. Soon after this the Southern Region began the planning for what was referred to as the 'ten-car scheme' whereby platform lengths were extended over much of the South Eastern commuter lines so allowing for longer trains to be operated in the hope of reducing congestion. Meanwhile there was still the occasional steam visitor to Cannon Street which may explain the presence of the mineral wagon – for ashes perhaps – on the left hand side.

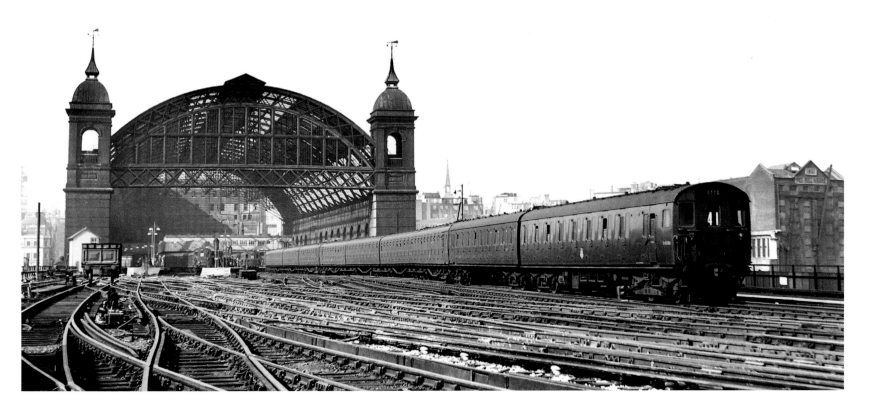

BR Standard 9F 2-10-0 No 92058 heads south from Elstree Tunnel on 25 May 1957, hauling loaded coal wagons from Nottingham for Cricklewood. Known to some crews as 'spaceships', this nickname came about because of the remarkable prowess of the design, arguably the finest of all the BR Standard types and that is not to say the others were bad either. Despite their small wheels they also had the ability to run fast, exceeding 90mph on several occasions, that is until a decree from Headquarters dictated their use on passenger workings – excepting the Somerset and Dorset – to cease as at speed they could cause significant track damage. At 90mph plus, the wheel rotational speed on one of these engines was also faster than those of *Mallard* when it had reached 126 mph back in 1938.

Passing the magnificent array of semaphore signals controlled by Greenock Princes Pier signal box, Pickersgill Caledonian Railway '928' class 3P 4-4-0 No 54468 marshalls empty coaching stock to form a train from Princes Pier station for Glasgow St Enoch on 22 June 1957. This is another example of cascading a locomotive from what had once been fast express duties to lesser tasks. Almost all the pre-grouping railways in the UK had operated 4-4-0 wheel arrangement engines at the start of the 20th century but these had been replaced on front line duties as train weights and speeds increased.

RIGHT Hauling loaded hoppers to Wellingborough, Franco-Crosti boilered Class 9F 2-10-0 No 92026 passes between Mill Hill Broadway and Elstree on 26 May 1957. A small number of the 9F type were fitted with a pre-heater under the main boiler – identified by the lower opening door. Exhaust gases would then pass through these before being ejected from a chimney on the side of the boiler, the conventional chimney being sealed and only used when lighting up from cold. The theory was that by pre-heating the boiler water a greater efficiency could be achieved as indeed had been demonstrated on steam engines operating in Italy. Unfortunately the same results were not found in the UK mainly due to the better design of the steam engine generally. Consequently the Franco-Crosti boilers were eventually replaced with those of a conventional type and the more normal chimney re-used. Smoke deflectors were never fitted to the engines either in the form seen here or later.

ABOVE Attached permanently to a somewhat makeshift wooden tender, Holmes North British 1882-designed Class Y9 0-4-0ST No 68117 stands on shed at Kipps (65E) on 22 June 1957. Unlike a normal steam engine tender, this addition just carried coal rather than coal and water, the latter commodity catered for in the saddle tank atop the boiler. Notice the wagon type handbrake on the exterior of the tender. Without this tender attachment only a limited supply of coal would have been able to be carried on the footplate so restricting the sphere of activity and time available for shunting.

RIGHT Passing through Perth at dawn on 24 June 1957, WD 2-8-0 No 90705 heads for Dunfermline with a mixture of wooden-bodied and steel-sided coal wagons. The standard open wagon used on the railways had for many years been built with a wooden body and often with a wooden underframe as well. A considerable proportion of these were also privately owned by collieries, factors, or individual merchants. Around the time of BR the standard mineral wagon began to be introduced which had the advantage of a greater carrying capacity and also being far more robust. The disadvantage was that they were rarely fitted with the continuous brake hence train speeds remained generally slow.

ABOVE Drummond Highland Railway 1P 0-4-4T No 55053 undergoes repair inside Lochgorm Works, Inverness, on 24 June 1957. The last examples of the Highland Railway engine fleet to remain in service, the two engines of the class were retained to work the branch line from Dornoch to The Mound. Both were withdrawn in the year that this scene was recorded. The lack of a smokebox numberplate may be noted and with no apparent fixing holes visible either. Was one in fact ever carried in BR days?

RIGHT With its only classmate No 61700 being named *Bantam Cock*, it was probably inevitable that No 61701, although not named, should be unofficially known as *Bantam Hen*. On 24 June 1957, it heads the 6.25am 'trip' freight from Aberdeen Yard to Laurencekirk. Class J39/3 0-6-0 No 64975 is alongside. Notice too the shunting pole laid across the front buffer beam of No 64975.

Amidst a smokescreen over the station, rebuilt 'Royal Scot' 4-6-0 No 46108 *Seaforth Highlander* restarts the 10.35am Leeds City-Glasgow St Enoch express from the Kilmarnock stop on 29 June 1957. In the background two former Midland Railway locos, 2Ps most likely, await their own respective departures.

Ex-LMS 2P 4-4-0 No 40597 pulls away from Kilmarnock on 29 June 1957, heading the 4.16pm train from Kilmarnock to Glasgow St Enoch. This engine is certainly well away from its original haunts on the Midland main line but has clearly found a new home in Scotland at 67B, Murlford, which came under the principal depot of Corkerhill. Again, notice the depot name painted on the bufferbeam to supplement the cast shed plate.

Allocated to Crewe North shed (5A), unrebuilt 'Patriot' 4-6-0 No 45546 *Fleetwood* is reversed on the Camden Town (1B) turntable on 6 July 1958; the shed in the background containing 'Black 5' 4-6-0 No 44942, 'Duchess' 46238 *City of Carlisle*, rebuilt 'Patriot' No 45528 and Caprotti 5MT 4-6-0 No 44752. This was a vacuum operated turntable, hence the connecting pipe. When ready the driver would open the ejector in the same way as if he were expelling air from the train pipe, after which the table could be turned without the need for human power although it will be noted there remain handles in case of emergency.

Moving to the far west now, we see much rebuilt Beattie L&SWR Class 0298 2-4-0 Well Tank No 30586 shunting at Wadebridge on 10 May 1958. The station here closed in 1967. Three of these diminutive tank engines were retained for use on the Wenford Bridge mineral line, the class when introduced originally used on London suburban duties – before electrification that is. Nearly all their time was now spent on the former duties although one was required daily for a school passenger service. The barrows on the platform were a regular feature at almost every station for decades. Spanning the tracks is a typical Southern Railway concrete footbridge.

ABOVE The 7.22am service from King's Cross to Hertford North climbs away from Copenhagen Tunnel on 24 July 1958, hauled by Class N2/2 0-6-2T No 69574. The formation is one of the articulated sets of carriages operating on the lines out of King's Cross and which were a feature to the end of steam working. Such fixed formations allowed regular travellers to almost 'bag' their own regular seat and woe-betide a stranger who dared take an 'allotted' space.

BELOW Type 4 Co-Co (later Class 40) No D202 passes Bethnal Green on 6 August 1958, powering the 3.45pm train from Norwich to Liverpool Street. Despite the 'modern' motive power a steam type headcode is still carried whilst the formation includes at least two LNER coaches. These diesel engines were some of the first main line locomotives production built for British Railways and, whilst unable to match the all out power of steam with an engine in good condition, good coal and a willing fireman, their 2,000hp power capacity was available all day and every day. The doors at the front were provided in the belief that multiple working might occur and access could then be required to the 'inner workings' en-route. In practise they were rarely if ever used.

'Black 5' 4-6-0 No 44916 heads briskly away from Stafford on 7 August 1958 with the 11.35 Blackpool-Birmingham train, unusually consisting of only three coaches. The impressive exhaust was more for the camera than the load! Assuming no additional vehicles were to be collected on the way, the crew should have an easy trip.

Class 3F 'Jinty' 0-6-0 No 47649 shunts the once extensive yards at Stafford on 11 August 1958. Shunting duties were the route to the main line for all footplate men. Cleaner, Passed Cleaner (meaning able to be called upon for firing) Fireman, Passed Fireman, and eventually Driver. Seniority in each grade also played its part as time was spend gaining experience on all types of working from shunting to local goods, distance working, passenger and eventually express passenger trains. Very different indeed to how things are in the 21st century.

The prototype Deltic passes Stafford on 11 August 1958, powering 'The Manxman' express from Liverpool Lime Street to Euston. The Deltic diesel was a revolution for its time when introduced as a private venture by English Electric in 1955. Using a pair of Napier 1,650hp engines, the power available was unlike anything that had been available to rail beforehand and which led the way to BR purchasing twenty-two Deltic types, having slight modifications from that seen here, for use on the Eastern Region in 1961. Here they reigned supreme, replacing steam until they too were usurped by the InterCity 125 sets.

ABOVE 28xx class 2-8-0 No 2883 passes through Stratford-upon-Avon station on 6 August 1958, hauling a freight working to Severn Tunnel Junction. This is almost certainly returning mineral empties to South Wales, the train taking the route through to Cheltenham, and thence via Gloucester and Lydney. Notice the first three wagons appear to be coke wagons, timber sided and again probably ex-private-owner stock. Further back are more modern steel mineral wagons.

RIGHT Jubilee class 4-6-0 No 45601 *British Guiana* powers up Camden Bank from Euston on 7 October 1958, with an express for Crewe, and passes BR Standard 4MT 2-6-4T No 80068 hauling empty coaching stock for Camden Yard. The Jubilee will just be starting on its journey and is evidently performing well with full boiler pressure as witness the amount of steam just escaping from the safety valves. The fireman has evidently done his work well for he has time to stand and observe.

ABOVE Leeds Neville Hill (50B)-based 'A3' Pacific No 60084 *Trigo* pulls away from Harrogate on 22 May 1959, with the 'Queen of Scots' Pullman, bound for London King's Cross. The LNER and later the Eastern Region ran a number of Pullman only trains, several surviving well into the diesel era. Not only was the standard fare payable but there was also a supplement for Pullman travel dependent upon whether first or second class Pullman was chosen. For this premium there was a meals-at-seat service (extra of course) and with generally accepted premium fare. There was no compunction to partake of food but it took strong willpower to ignore the aroma of the steward passing with food – perhaps to serve one's fellow passengers.

LEFT Fitted with a double chimney, 'A3' Pacific No 60050 *Persimmon* departs from York on 22 May 1959, hauling an express from Newcastle to King's Cross. The roundhouse is York South shed, a subsidiary to York (50A) and not given a shed code of its own. Track rationalisation at York has reduced the amount of rails seen here considerably in recent years, whilst within the train shed the most obvious change has to be the removal of the centre through lines. The roundhouse too is sadly no more.

RIGHT With double summertime in force, the 9.20pm train for Rolleston Junction awaits departure from Southwell on 23 May 1959, behind ex-Midland Class 1P 0-4-4T No 58065. Local services such as these often provided feeder workings into main line services although by the 1950s many were simply not paying their way. It remains ironic that politicians from different generations and parties have long waxed lyrical about the benefits of an integrated transport policy; we had one years ago with feeder services such as these, and it was those same politicians who allowed the same to fade away.

ABOVE The King's Cross-bound 'Talisman' express passes Selby on 23 May 1959, headed by 'A2' class Pacific No 60539 *Bronzino*. This was another class with connections to racehorses in some of their names, *Sugar Palm*, *Irish Elegance* and *Blue Peter* to name but three. Other names were based more on the traditional *Robert the Bruce*, *Waverley* and *A. H. Peppercorn*, the latter named after the last Chief Mechanical Engineer of the LNER. One of the type was saved for scrap, *Blue Peter*, the purchase price of buying the engine from BR greatly assisted with the help of children who watched the BBC children's programme of the same name.

ABOVE The 'Blue Belle' special from London Victoria to the Bluebell Railway ran on 15 September 1963, behind LSWR-liveried T9 class 4-4-0 No 120 and Caledonian Railway 4-2-2 No 123. Passing near Balcombe, the train here makes the return journey to the London terminus. After a lapse of several decades, through running to and from the Bluebell Railway is once again possible but now via East Grinstead instead of Ardingly. Both steam and diesel excursions have taken the East Grinstead connection in recent times and whilst both the engines seen here still survive today it is extremely unlikely there would ever be a repeat of this type of motive power on a modern day special.

LEFT Descending the incline from Finsbury Park, Class 31 No D5640 heads for King's Cross with a motley collection of empty coaching stock to form the 'Sheffield Pullman' departure. In the formation of both pre-war Pullman cars and the more modern Metropolitan Cammell variant, the latter consists solely of Parlour cars as no brake vehicles of this type were even built.

BELOW At the old Euston on 27 July 1957, Oerlikon stock awaits departure, forming a local service to Watford, and 2P 4-4-0 No 40683 has arrived with a semi-fast from Northampton. The original Euston was often said to be tired, dirty and confusing to passengers. The latter may well have been the case but the first two hardly apply here, the platform area spick and span whilst the glass roof even gives an airy appearance. Perhaps it was the passengers who dragged it down

Passing through Princes Street Gardens, and approaching Edinburgh Waverley station on 8 August 1958, an original Gloucester RC&W twin DMU, with DMBS No Sc51112 on the rear, operates a cross-city suburban service between Corstorphine and Rosewell & Hawthornden. The latter station closed for traffic in September 1962, while Corstorphine remained open until January 1968. This was one of the early DMU vehicle combinations intended to modernise suburban and branch line operation. The initial fleet were acquired from a variety of builders and as such were not always electrically and mechanically compatible, resulting in some early casualties. The Gloucester vehicles were not one of these and achieved a reasonable lifespan with some serving almost thirty years in traffic. Three survive in preservation.

Post-steam and climbing Holloway Bank towards Finsbury Park on 22 March 1972, Brush Type 4 (later Class 47) No 1969 heads a Cambridge Buffet Express from King's Cross. For a time at least it seemed as if almost every second passenger train would have a CL47 at its head, the example seen here still sporting its original two-tone green livery albeit with full yellow ends and four digit number. The engine was renumbered 47791 and when taken out of service was scrapped in 2013.

Class 411/2 4CEP No 7129 emerges from Chislehurst Tunnel at Elmstead Woods on 16 May 1974, leading the 13.10 train from Charing Cross to Margate. The provision of a corridor connection and the overhung roof probably epitomised the best looking SR EMU sets for many years. The CEP units were introduced ready for the Kent Coast Electrification, the first phase of which commenced in 1959. Prior to this long lines of brand new units were stored in open countryside between Haywards Heath and Ardingly and apparently with almost no vandalism occurring.

Class 86 No E3154 (later No 86255 *Penrith Beacon*) climbs Camden Bank on 16 May 1973 with an express from London Euston to Manchester Piccadilly, and rapidly overtakes No E3139 of the same class (later No 86257 *Snowdon*) with empty coaching stock for the washing plant. Electric traction had made the climbing of Camden bank, and further north the ascents of Beattock and Grayrigg, easy compared with steam days, "…turn the handle and off we go…" was the term used, the whole achieved by the driver whilst comfortably sat down in front of his control desk.

The Euston-bound 'Emerald Isle Express' emerges from Primrose Hill Tunnel and begins the descent of Camden Bank on 6 June 1973, headed by Class 86 No E3106, later No 86214 *SansPareil*. This was the 'modern' railway of the period and so different to the scene just a decade earlier. Blue and grey livery had helped to transform the image although the choice of blue remains open to debate with those in the know admitting it was the worst choice of colour for wear.

Class 74 No E6106 passes through Clapham Cutting on 15 August 1973, powering the 06.18 service from Weymouth to Waterloo. The Class 74 electro-diesel locomotives were a rebuild for the Bournemouth electrification and intended for boat train use as well as ordinary locomotive hauled services. Away from electrified routes their 600hp diesel engine was sufficient for low speed operation although no doubt it will be working on 'the juice' here. These rebuilds were never an unqualified success and amongst the nicknames given for the design (some unsuitable to be reproduced here) was that of 'spin-dryers' based on the fact that the diesel engine once started would run up to and remain at full revolutions.

On the many occasions that I visited Holloway Bank, this was the one and only time that I managed to record a train on the viaduct at the same time as one came underneath. On 12 September 1972, Class 55 'Deltic' No 9007 Pinza emerges from Copenhagen Tunnel with the 17.30 express for Bradford and Halifax, as an electrification train crosses above, returning to King's Cross yards behind Class 31 No 5800.

Vale of Rheidol 2-6-2T No 8 *Llywelyn* about to depart from Devils Bridge on 4 October 1973, heading the 15.45 V of R service to Aberystwyth. For a time the three steam engines operating this line appeared in standard blue with the double arrow symbol as seen here. It was not a successful combination for steam and there was a considerable sigh of relief when a revision to more appropriate colours was made. Notice the bulbous casing to the left of the lamp on the rear; this was to allow room for the handle of the handbrake to be rotated when necessary.

ABOVE On 13 June 1974, the 09.12 'Tees-Tyne Pullman' from Newcastle to London King's Cross departs from Darlington, powered by Class 55 Deltic No 55011 *The Royal Northumberland Fusiliers*. The Pullman rake is of modern vehicles but with a BR Mk1 full brake in standard blue/grey livery at each end. Pullman at the time had a reversal of the corporate colours meaning the colour scheme was grey/blue. The lighter colouring was nearest the solebar; not the best combination and where it was prone to show dirt and brake dust.

OPPOSITE TOP Passing the site of Ripon Line Junction, south of Thirsk, on 13 June 1974, Class 40s Nos 40124 (allocated to Wigan Springs Branch) and No 40159, from Haymarket, head an unidentified northbound train. To repeat a photograph from this position today, a veritable forest would have to be cleared.

OPPOSITE BOTTOM A Liverpool-Hull Class 124/1 Trans-Pennine DMU stands in Platform 1 at Selby on 14 June 1974, and is passed on the through line by Class 37s Nos 37085 & 37216 with a haul of down coal hoppers. The Class 37 type had proven to be one of the most versatile of all BR designs and some still survive in the service of the private operators in 2019. External variations in body styling also existed such as here with split headcode boxes, deemed necessary to allow access between locomotives via the front doors. In practice they were rarely used and few crew members shed a tear when the doors were permanently sealed so reducing instances of draughts within the cab area.

EM1 Class 76 Bo-Bo No 76050 near Dinting on 14 June 1974, hauling westbound loaded coal hoppers. These electric locomotives operated on the 1,500Vdc overhead system and were also fitted with regenerative braking, meaning when the brakes were applied the heat generated was converted back into electrical energy and fed back into the catenary wire.

The 15.50 Boat Train for Waterloo awaits departure from Weymouth Quay on 1 July 1974, headed by Class 33/1 'Crompton' No 33107. Weymouth Quay has ceased to welcome trains for some years now but at the time the passage of a train along which was in effect a public road was also fraught as inconsiderate motorists would park their cars preventing the passage of the train. Railwaymen became experts at moving vehicles out of the way…!

Class 71 No 71006 traverses the Chislehurst-St Mary Cray Loop on 28 August 1974, hauling a transfer freight from the Eastern Region to Dover. The Class 71 straight-electric locos were the original design from which the CL74 type later evolved. Introduced from 1959 onwards, they were used mainly on non-passenger and freight but also took turns on the 'Golden Arrow' and 'Night Ferry' workings commensurate with the full electrification of the Kent Coast main lines from 1961 onwards. Notice the single pantograph on the roof, raised in certain areas where the provision of the third rail could have proved dangerous to shunters and other staff and in consequence where limited overhead wire collection was available.

Class 71 No 71002 awaits departure from London Victoria on 17 September 1974, heading the 02.55 Newspaper train to Maidstone. Newspaper traffic was then a regular and lucrative traffic for the railway and one which was also given priority. The small hours at almost every London terminus would see the newspaper vans arrive accompanied by jostling and shouting as 'hurry up' calls emanated from all round. Sadly it is a traffic that has been lost, but then with internet news now instantaneous the need would have diminished anyway.

ABOVE Deltic No 55001 *St Paddy* awaits departure from King's Cross on 6 December 1974 with the 22.15 'Night Aberdonian'. Night photography required both preparation and forethought whilst a clear night was also necessary. The JCB nearby is no doubt ready for some civil engineering work and is certainly not the selected motive power for the next departure!

RIGHT Class 71 No 71005 purrs to itself at London Victoria in the small hours of 17 September 1974, awaiting departure with the 03.00 newspaper train to Dover Western Docks.

ABOVE The 04.27 china clay empties (6V53) from Stoke-on-Trent to St Blazey emerges from Parsons Tunnel, near Teignmouth, on 8 August 1975, hauled by Class 52 No 1041 *Western Prince*, a loco now preserved on the East Lancs Railway. This of course is the province of the famed Dawlish sea wall and where walkers could be seen (weather permitting) almost every day of the year. The locomotive is in its last months of service, the Westerns falling by the wayside whenever a defect occurred that was not immediately able to be rectified.

RIGHT The 09.30 train to Cambridge winds out of Platform 2 at King's Cross on 12 June 1975, hauled by Class 31/4 No 31401. The first vehicle will be noted as a Buffet car and so is hardly ideally placed for the convenience of passengers.

Having checked the couplings, the guard climbs into the cab of Class 71 No 71011 in Hither Green yard on 25 February 1976, prior to the loco hauling its load to Chatham. The pantograph will be lowered as soon as the loco transfers to third rail power.

A rake of Murco tanks approaches Reading from the north on 7 April 1976, hauled by Class 47/0 No 47004. The train may have originated from Avonmouth in which case they will be full tanks or alternatively these might well be empty cars on the way back to Fawley for refilling. In both cases nowadays much fuel is now sent by underground pipeline and trains such as these are becoming a rarity.

ABOVE Class 08 No 08387 takes oil tanks into Eastleigh yards from an earlier freight arrival on 3 May 1976. The yard is to the right of the image whilst it will also be noted there is a Class 33 locomotive at the opposite end of the train. Consequently it is slightly unusual in that the train is being drawn back rather than having entered the yard under its own power. Might it have been that the Class 33 had failed and the train was being moved off the main line rather than block a running line?

RIGHT On the Bluebell Railway on 15 May 1976, West Country Pacific No 21C123 *Blackmore Vale*, replete with 'Atlantic Coast Express' headboard, climbs Freshfield Bank with a service from Sheffield Park to Horstead Keynes.

Ford Motor Company containers for Dagenham are powered through Bushey on 30 June 1976 by Class 85 No 85012. This is the type of block working which has replaced the traditional freight working. A train for one customer intended for a single destination. Industry was also changing its working practices with certain parts now built in dedicated factories rather than each factory working independently.

Class 25 No 25174 heads towards Watford Tunnel and Watford Junction on 30 June 1976, hauling a southbound block working of Tunnel Cement Co hoppers.

Class 50 No 50020 *Revenge* crosses the Royal Albert Bridge at Saltash on 19 September 1975, with the 11.00 Plymouth-Penzance train. The Class 50 locomotives had been built as replacements for the Class 40s principally on the West Coast main line. Following full electrification of the route they were cascaded to the Western Region where together with the CL47 they usurped the remaining Warship and Western classes on top link passenger duty. With the introduction of the HST they took their final passengers on the Waterloo-Exeter trains although as years passed reliability suffered and we know the then Southern Region general manager, Gordon Pettit, was pleased to see them replaced with modern DMUs.

On the Romney Hythe & Dymchurch Railway on 15 August 1976, Davey Paxman Pacific No 1 *Green Goddess* pulls away from Hythe station, bound for Dungeness.

ABOVE A three-car BRCW Class 104/1 DMU, with DMCL No M50527 leading, approaches Manchester Victoria from Red Bank sidings as empty stock to form a service for Blackpool North on 22 September 1976. At this time, members of the class regularly working Blackpool diagrams were given a white band below the bodyside windows.

LEFT Class 20s Nos 20127 & 20017 pass through the old Rotherham station on 21 September 1976, heading a train of steel coil for Sheffield. A pair of Class 20 types were usually semi-permanently coupled in the way seen here and in which form driver visibility was far better than being restricted to a small side window followed by a long engine casing.

ABOVE Class 25 No 25050 arrives at Gleneagles on 28 May 1977, heading the 13.38 service from Dundee to Glasgow Queen Street. Some staff evidently still took pride in their station gardens.

LEFT Formed of Class 502 'Southport' EMUs and led by Driving Car No M28341M, the 11.44 train to Ormskirk departs from Liverpool Exchange on 23 September 1976.

A southbound mixed freight passes through Carrbridge on 31 May 1977, headed by Class 40 No 40001. Notice the railman seemingly engaged in painting white marks on the edge of the platform.

Index